SOIL

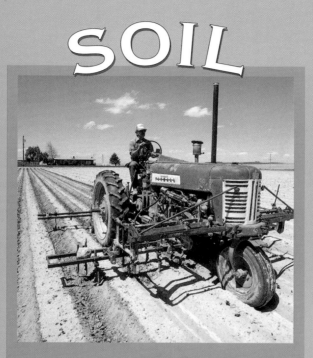

A TRUE BOOK

by
Christin Ditchfield

Children's Press®
A Division of Scholastic Inc.

New York Toronto London Auckland Sydney
Mexico City New Delhi Hong Kong
Danbury, Connecticut

Children plant a tree in soil.

Content Consultant
Jan Jenner, Ph.D.

Reading Consultant
Linda Cornwell
National Literacy Specialist

Library of Congress Cataloging-in-Publication Data

Ditchfield, Christin.
    Soil / by Christin Ditchfield.
        p. cm. — (A True book)
    Includes bibliographical references and index.
    ISBN 0-516-22344-5 (lib. bdg.)   0-516-29368-0 (pbk.)
    1. Soils—Juvenile literature. 2. Soil ecology—Juvenile literature.
[1. Soils. 2. Soil ecology. 3. Ecology.] I. Title. II. Series.
S591.3 .D58 2002
631.4—dc21

                                                              2001023107

Contents

You probably walk over soil every day without even thinking about it!

What Is Soil?

Soil is nearly everywhere you look! A thin coating of soil covers most of the Earth's dry land surface. In some places the soil is only a few inches deep. In other places, it may be several feet deep. Some people call it dirt or earth, but soil is more than just the ground you walk on. Soil is really one of our most valuable natural resources! A natural resource is a substance found in nature that has many important uses.

Houses, schools, and factories are built on soil. Soil lies underneath the roads you walk and drive on. It can be found at the bottom of every lake, river, and ocean.

Workers build a home on soil.

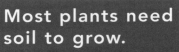

Most plants need soil to grow.

Flowers and trees grow in soil. So do fruits and grains and vegetables. In fact, farmers grow most of the foods you eat in fields that are full of good, rich soil. Without soil, few plants could grow. The Earth would be a rocky planet! Soil stores the water, air, and **nutrients** that living plants need.

Many animals make their homes in the soil. Mice,

Many foxes make their
homes out of soil.

rabbits, foxes, and prairie dogs tunnel into the dirt to make their homes. All kinds of worms, mites, and insects live in the soil, as well. (A mite is a tiny eight-legged animal that is related to spiders.) Scientists tell us that there may be as many as 5,000 insects living in 1 square foot (0.09 square meter) of soil!

The soil itself is made up of many different ingredients.

This close-up photograph shows bacillus cerus, a type of bacteria commonly found in soil.

This mixture includes water, air, rocks, clay, sand, and material from plants and animals that have rotted away and fallen apart. Soil also holds tiny creatures called **bacteria** and fungi. These creatures help to break down the dead plant and animal material into very small pieces.

Digging Deeper

The soil you see all around took many years to form. It started out as solid rock. Over time, wind, rain, and freezing and thawing wore the rock down into small pieces. Animals and people stepped on the rock, breaking it into smaller pieces. Plants grew nearby and sent

Plants grew in the cracks in the rocks.

down roots that broke through any little cracks in the rock. Eventually, the tiny pieces of

15

This photograph shows the different layers of soil in the ground.

rock were covered by dead plant and animal material. This is how soil begins.

If you could dig deep below the surface of the Earth, you would see that soil forms in different layers. Each of these flat layers is called a horizon. When **geologists** study all the layers of soil in a particular place, they call their study a soil profile.

The most visible layer
of soil is the topsoil.

The topsoil is the layer of
soil that you can see on the
surface. It may be less than an

inch thick or as deep as a foot. Topsoil feels loose and soft. It looks darker than any other layer of soil, because it is the richest and holds the most humus. Humus is a mixture of rotting leaves, dead plants, and animal waste. Worms, snails, and insects live in the topsoil. Many eat the small pieces of plant material, turning it into even smaller pieces. Millions of bacteria live in the topsoil, too. They break down

the waste material even further. Gardeners plant their seeds in topsoil, because it has the nutrients that plants need to grow well.

Underneath the topsoil is the subsoil. This layer is usually thicker—anywhere from several inches to several feet deep. Subsoil looks lighter because it

Subsoil is a lighter color than topsoil.

has less humus in it. Fewer living creatures make their way to the subsoil. This dirt is much more tightly packed. It contains slightly bigger pieces of rock. Only large bushes and trees are strong enough to push their roots down through the subsoil.

Big, coarse rocks mix with a little soil to form the fragmented rock layer. Nothing can grow at this level. Under the fragmented rock you will

An excavator removes loose rock to uncover the bedrock layer.

find the deepest layer, the solid bedrock. This layer is the original rock on which the soil began to form.

Types of Soil

There are many different kinds of soil. Soil may be brown, black, or even red! Some soil feels rough. Other soil feels soft. The texture, or feel, of the soil depends on the type of rock that the soil came from. Scientists tell us that all types of soil have a mixture

Soil can be many different colors.

of three main ingredients, which are sand, silt, and clay.

The soil in this area in South Africa is mostly sandy.

Soil that is mostly made of sand feels gritty or rough. If you look at it closely, you will see small pieces of broken rock. Sandy soil is the heaviest soil. It dries quickly after the rain. Soil that contains a lot of silt is grainy. It also has little pieces of rock in it, but you would need a magnifying glass to see them. Silty soil takes longer to dry than sandy soil.

Soil that has more clay in it feels slippery smooth. Clay

The soil in Georgia has lots of clay particles, giving it a reddish color.

particles are the smallest and lightest of all soil particles. The pieces of rock are so tiny that they cannot be seen. The biggest clay particle is five hundred times smaller than a single grain of sand! This type of soil gets sticky and muddy when it is wet. It takes the longest time to dry.

When soil has equal amounts of sand and silt, with a little bit of clay mixed in, scientists call it loam. Plants grow best in loam, because this soil holds just the right amount of nutrients, water, and air.

Check It Out!

Soil is a mixture made of different materials. Here is an experiment that will help you see the separate ingredients in your soil.

You need:

Soil

A large jar with a lid

Water

A large spoon or small shovel

1. Scoop some soil into the jar until the jar is about one-third full.

2. Add water until the jar is full. Put the lid on tightly. Shake the jar carefully for 15 to 20 seconds.

3. Leave the jar in a safe place overnight. In the morning, look at the layers of soil in your jar. Do you see the different colors and textures?

Usually the bottom layer will include sand and small rocks—the heaviest ingredients in soil. Next you'll find silt, and then clay particles near the top.

What Is Next?

Soil is an important part of everyday life. We need to protect soil from harm and use it wisely. People have not always taken good care of this resource.

The roots of trees and plants help hold soil in its place. However, people have cut

We rely on soil for much of our food supply.

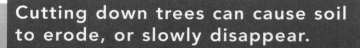
Cutting down trees can cause soil to erode, or slowly disappear.

down thousands and thousands of trees in order to build things. Farmers dig up the grass, trees, and bushes in a field so that they can plant crops. This can lead to soil **erosion**, when the soil is blown away by wind or washed away by rain.

Soil can also be damaged by poisonous chemicals. These chemicals get spilled in garbage dumps, where they pollute the earth. Farmers

Some farmers use planes to spray chemicals on their crops. These chemicals may get into the soil and cause problems.

often use chemicals to kill weeds and **fertilize** crops. Some of these chemicals can be harmful to people, plants, and animals. Poisons in the soil may seep into our rivers and lakes.

Scientists are working to find ways to save our soil. They have designed safer garbage dumps that keep poisonous chemicals from leaking into the soil.

A scientist studies a soil sample.

Recycling garbage, such as aluminum cans, helps protect the soil.

People all over the world have started to **recycle** their garbage and re-use it— instead of sending it to garbage dumps. Volunteers plant bushes and trees to replace the ones that have been cut down. Many farmers now use special methods to grow crops and keep the soil healthy at the same time. They use chemicals that are safe or none at all.

A boy makes compost, which can be used in a garden to make the soil richer.

Some families collect dead leaves and plants and kitchen scraps in compost containers. This compost becomes humus, which enriches the soil. Working together, people are learning to take good care of the soil. After all, it is not just dirt— it is an important natural resource!

Fun Fact About Soil

Did you know that earthworms have a very important job? They are part of nature's recycling team. When earthworms dig their tunnels underground, they mix the layers of soil together. The tunnels let fresh air and water down into the soil.

When an earthworm nibbles on decaying leaves and flowers, it releases the vitamins and **minerals** that are inside the old plants into the soil. This makes the soil healthier for the new plants that will grow in it.

To Find Out More

Here are some additional resources to help you learn more about soil:

 **Books**

Glaser, Linda. **Compost! Growing Gardens From Your Garbage.** The Millbrook Press, 1996.

Gordon, Mike and Maria. **Simple Science Rocks and Soil.** Raintree Steck-Vaughn Publishers, 1996.

Manci, William E. **Farming and the Environment.** Gareth Stevens Publishing, 1993.

Richardson, Joy. **Rocks and Soil.** Franklin Watts, 1992.

Sneddon, Robert. **The Super Science Book of Rocks and Soils.** Thomson Learning, 1995.

Stille, Darlene R. **Soil Erosion and Pollution.** Children's Press, 1990.

American Geological Institute
4220 King Street
Alexandria, VA 22302
http://www.agiweb.org

This organization provides information on the geosciences, and offers scholarships, mentoring, and school materials on earth science for grades K–12.

Natural Resources Conservation Service
http://www.nrcs.usda.gov

This federal agency works in partnership with the American people to conserve and sustain our natural resources. Includes special web pages for teachers and students.

Planetpals Earthzone
http://www.planetpals.com

This online site provides facts about the Earth and recycling as well as games and puzzles.

Soil Science Society of America
677 South Segoe Road
Madison, WI 53711
http://www.soils.org

This society studies crop production, environmental issues, waste management, recycling, and wise land use.

United States Environmental Protection Agency
Explorers' Club for Kids
http://www.epa.gov/kids/

This website combines facts with fun—games, contests, and ways you can help protect the environment.

Important Words

bacteria living creatures that have only one cell and are too tiny to be seen without a microscope

erosion the process where soil is gradually carried away by water, wind, or ice

fertilize adding something to soil to help plants grow

geologist a scientist who studies rocks, minerals, and fossils to learn about the Earth

mineral a non-living substance found in nature that is necessary to the health and well-being of living things

nutrient something needed by people, plants, and animals in order to stay healthy

particle an extremely small part of something

recycle to save and use over again

Index

Meet the Author

Christin Ditchfield is the author of a number of books for Children's Press, including five True Books on Natural Resources. A former elementary school teacher, she is now a freelance writer and conference speaker, and host of the nationally syndicated radio program, *Take It To Heart!* Ms. Ditchfield makes her home in Sarasota, Florida.